A COAT OF ASHES

By the same author:

Coracle: poems 1991–2007 (2009)
q finger (chapbook) (2011)
lemon oil (2013)

A COAT OF ASHES

JACKSON

RECENT
WORK
PRESS

A coat of ashes
Recent Work Press
Canberra, Australia

Copyright © Janet Ruth Jackson, 2019

ISBN: 9780648404231 (paperback)

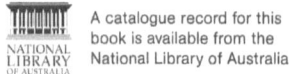
A catalogue record for this
book is available from the
National Library of Australia

All rights reserved. This book is copyright. Except for private study, research, criticism or reviews as permitted under the Copyright Act, no part of this book may be reproduced, stored in a retrieval system, or transmitted in any form by any means without prior written permission. Enquiries should be addressed to the publisher.

Cover image: 'Computer simulation of the growth of cosmic structure' © 2005 The Millennium Simulation, Springel et al. (Virgo Consortium), Max Planck Insitute for Astrophysics. Reproduced with permission.
Cover design by Recent Work Press
Set by Recent Work Press

recentworkpress.com

Contents

The silicon lip of the precipice	1
One, two, three	2
it happened	4
The light	6
skinvisible	9
Touched all over	11
William, an elegy	12
On eating shepherd's pie from a plastic takeaway box	13
white furniture	15
between	16
The other way, the long way	17
lamps	19
That	20
The Millennium Simulation	21
[ ]	22
between the bones of my temples	23
Wake	25
Enlightenment	29
A coat of ashes	30
I cut my hair short	31
The huge word	32
The centre	34
The nothing	38
That girdle!	41
on the path	42
The Sage and the Physicist	43
The fundamental forces dream	44
the analogy	45
The upper bound	47
dào kě dào fēi cháng dào	50
trace	51
Spangles	52
The socks surrender	53
a beach	54

That vast sea	55
Selective Logging	56
Corpse Pose	58
to matter & thrum	59
Turning off time	60
At the University Library	62
Thirteen ways of looking at an unseen bird	64
Meditation	65
Calculus	66
What is Tao?	67
her wings	68
The soft split	69
The catbeing	70
Turnings	72
Returning to the root	73
A dumb Daoist	74
Open an eye at the surface	76
The tiny echo	79
On looking at the Pointers	80
Afterword	82

The silicon lip of the precipice

In my dream there wasn't a magpie
warbling caroling arguing garbling
back and forth back and forth
with another about resources

There wasn't a lorikeet,
shrieking competing wreaking clichéd
havoc in the last remaining
clichéd freaking shivering tuart trees

There wasn't a raven
hahring and harking electric on the lines,
calling conversing drak, black, smack,
crack on the concrete lawns

In my dream there weren't sixteen
lightly birded hedged picketed lines
There was only the edge of everything
The silicon lip of the precipice and you

on it
with your eyes
like the ice that's about to melt,
and in your grip

a broken bottle, its razor neck
like a talon or a hooked beak,
bald as a silver dollar
or a Jolly Roger, you

on it
with your eyes
warding off my tooth and clichéd
nail and greedy breathing

One, two, three

The child can't do a cartwheel.
She can do a headstand, a handstand,
but a cartwheel needs momentum, a swinging centre
of gravity. The child doesn't know
momentum, centres, gravity.
She blames her mother's

ski-slope lawn, fenced off in the middle
of a hillside farm. Far below the river lurks
among giant trees. Far above is the boundary fence
and the forested climb she completed once
to peep at the house on top. Her father calls
its owner mad. When she does a handstand

the child doesn't think of the river,
the trees, the mountain, the madman.
She thinks green blades,
soft-sharp, flattening
under fingers. Ants. Beetles.
Her father mows the grass

infrequently. It spreads thick runners, yellow-white,
with bright chlorophyll arrowheads. Her father talks
war at them, but he's not a fighter. The child
can do a headstand, a handstand
but never thinks to think
if I can do that

I can turn a cartwheel. A cartwheel is only
a moving handstand. At school she sees the others
cartwheeling freely on the flat lawns.
Her father is the gardener. He keeps it
well, wanders in it like Wittgenstein. The others
make fun of him. The child watches

their cartwheels. Asks. One, two,
three, they laugh. But the child is not co-
ordinated. She doesn't have her count
together. The numbers come
in space, away
from tummy, hips,

knees. She tries again. Runs,
throws her hands down
to the grass, heaves her bottom over.
It isn't a cartwheel.
Never that flinging feeling.
Her legs will not go up and over. It needs

more force, she thinks.
Runs faster, heaves harder.
It never works.
Never at school
on the flat lawns in front
of everyone. Never on the scraggy

home slope, where the shape of things pulls her down,
away from the mountain and the madman's house,
down, down to the river,
and her mother is framed in the kitchen window
saying Be careful! Oh, do
be careful!

it happened

they died moaning   the structure
of their skins   failed

as I sat   above
the sea   in a human space
white chairs   white gravel
a high Hellenic shore
they came out   of the sea

the whales   bloated with water
moaning   a terrible noise the sea
emptying   of whales

the only survivors   were babies
in the dream   these babies had fur
saved   by brown fur
we were going to have to care
for them now   their mothers
were corpses   it happened

the same night   I saw
the rockets

there was a war
there's always a war
two or three seas away
gunships submarines   at
each other   but

as I   sat above
the sea   in a human space
white chairs white gravel
a high Hellenic shore
they came out   of the sea

just   there
in the bay   two rockets
shot out of the sea
a terrible noise
flew as high as a skyscraper
faltered   turned
dived   burning
into the sea   it happened

the same night   the whales

she said it was caused

the marine biologist
in her blue-piped khaki
overall said with her brown
ponytail said when I asked
no
it's not just here
it's global
all the whales
the whole world
at the same moment

it was   caused
by the war   she said

The light

The light has to get somewhere, touch something, to exist
You take acid as we're sitting in the air
The old woman pours whitewash over her husband's head
We're on the left
There's no box, no comfort zone
Anything but raw paper is a compromise
Two girls with acne and stringy bleached hair
Occupy Wall Street
A month in the hole
In solitary
The way to connect is to work together
I had a clear vision
Looming orange clouds, an apocalyptic sunset
Something that makes you smaller or channels your movement

The light has to get somewhere
A curve through spacetime
A function
A journey, transmission, idea
In the dream we're on a plane, rows of seats, going somewhere
We don't know what we want but it isn't this
People keep pets
The husband is grey and decrepit
If your mother couldn't hold you while you cried
hold yourself now
Try to hide yourself
If you throw up the next morning
does that mean you've poisoned yourself?
When you look for yourself as a thing
there is nothing there

The light has to get somewhere, touch something
Is that the same t-shirt?
Occupy Breastfeeding

Howl, keen, be the banshee of yourself, announcing your death
I take scissors out of your hand
You're taking acid
Seeing the nothing inside yourself
A curve through spacetime
A function
A journey, transmission, idea
In touching something, the light
is not destroyed, but changed
In the dream
the husband is grey and decrepit
The woman pours whitewash
Anything but raw paper is a compromise
The noises when I cried and cried frightened me

The light has to get somewhere, touch something, to exist
People keep pets instead
Curl into a ball, try to hide yourself
We don't know what we want but it isn't this
Fenced in, fenced out
You in the aisle seat
I in the middle
Light is nothing, only
potential
When you look for yourself as a thing
there is nothing
The way to connect is to work
against each other
In touching something, the light
is not destroyed, but changed
Reflected, absorbed, refracted
Tear at your clothes and hair, bite yourself

The light has to get somewhere
I smile a little
Acid, you're taking acid
Light is nothing, only

potential, just
an idea
Occupy Everything
Looming orange clouds
The window seat free
No-one looking out
This is not conditional
A month in the hole
Two months
Give you time to think
What if the neighbours come
and try to cheer me up?
Not depressed
Not ill
Don't need anything
In full control
of self, life, responses
An adult
Tear at your clothes and hair, bite yourself
I don't know what I want
If your father couldn't hold you while you cried
hold yourself now
In touching something, the light
is not destroyed, but changed
Polarised, amplified, focussed
There's no box
This is not
conditional
You don't have to be
a good boy, a good girl
I had a clear vision
The light
has to touch something

skinvisible

> *facing each other*
> *one truth apart*
> —Kevin Gillam

i this
   thing
      itchy with text

Your voice is an underground stream
hiding small eyeless creatures
Touching you is breaking something

again we
   pass
      masked
in black
   filmed
      skinvisible
the huge unsaid
   suspended
      wired

again we
   pass
      filmed
in black
   framed
      in bits
skinvisible
   maintain our com-
      position

particles ex-
   changed only

        in theory
      functions col-
        lapsed only
           in thought

Your voice is an underground stream
Touching you is

i this thing itchy
   with text
      breaking something

Touched all over

How does it feel, balancing on crammed
paws, coated
in killed fibres, lurching on two
long stilts,
your boulder head trying to fly?

How does it feel, sleeping in nests
so enormous and uncamouflaged,
so closed, inert and thick that they block
the smell of the Earth,
her dirt and cambium flesh, her whispers,
hoots, roars,
the liquid slap of her moon waves,
her leaf waves,
the broad spectrum given by the sun?

How does it feel to be touched all over
by nothing?

William, an elegy

He would raise his food between his forefeet and carefully bite into it.
His eyes on the sides of his head were obsidian planets.
He spoke only when in pain.
His snout was fringed with bursts of white whiskers.
He was an autopoietic system.
His many toes were long and pink, each with its claw.
His pink skin tail was as long as his body and faintly brushed with stiff translucent hairs.
He was a universe.
He was creamy white with black shoulders.
His fur was streamlined from teeth to tail-root.
He spoke only when in pain.
Humans kept him in a one-metre cage where he lived for two autumns, two springs.
Humans brought him edible pellets and shredded documents.
Humans squeaked at him, William, William.
He was an autopoietic system.
He made a warm familiar ratsmelling nest.
He stored some food for the winter.
He was a universe.
On the seventh day humans threw out everything he had and brought back the ink smell.
He made a warm familiar nest.
He stored some food.
On the seventh day humans threw out everything he had.
He made a warm nest.
He stored food.
On the seventh day humans threw out everything.

On eating shepherd's pie from a plastic takeaway box

Thank you for your flesh
I hope
a prayer was
said for your software
    as the abattoir crashed it
    with an electric bolt,
    unplugged it
    with a blade

Thank you for your muscle
I hope a ritual
farewelled
your memory, the shape
    of mother, two teats,
    woolled udder's
    press against nose
your process, the way
    your tail felt flicking,
    anus releasing its pebbles,
    heart leaping

I hope you
walked
    on grass
    among trees
    under sun
played, ran, chased,
lay down between warm bodies
    as stars flocked
    above you

Thank you for your membranes
I hope some words were spoken

to lay to rest
your script, the fear of
   dog, horror of ape,
   the vowel rising in your throat,
   the rush to follow the others
your inputs, the shove on your eardrums
   of shouts and motors,
     the force under cloven pointes
   of dirt, concrete, metal grid

When my instructions said *eat*
   your components were made
   available
Your salt, minerals, proteins
   are turning into
   my marrow
your fats and sugars
   powering
   my motion, my thought,
   my words
You becoming me, I
becoming you

as I sit
   on grass
   among trees
   under sun
licking the fangs of my
   plastic fork

and trying to make a prayer
   for

white furniture

Again I dreamed that complex edifice
For a while I'd had a bedsit in a rear wing
You locked your bike to a back-lane fence,
wended between outbuildings, climbed
fire escape, squirmed through window. Now

I was trying to move in to the top floor of the main block where
a lot of students and workers and a few retired eccentrics had
units in a group around a common room where people were
coming and going and leaving magazines lying about in too
many colours and flavours but all I wanted

was a tidy flat with white furniture
and blue bowls; a kitchen with everything
clean; a small fridge singing
efficiently; a living room with nothing

overstuffed. It was there, I knew,
somewhere within the clamour and mess,
waiting for my key. A plain door.

between

Driving between Pinjarra and Dwellingup, between
wire-fenced paddocks, stubble, wan dead logs,
I thought, what am I doing here? What am
I doing here? Then I thought,

blasting along at twenty-five metres per second,
raising no visible dust where I touch the
tarmac at four spinning steel-belted rubber
tangents, riding on air, I'm not

here. I'm actually not
here. Because I'd

slowed down
to make art,

two Recreational Vehicles loomed in my mirrors,
blurred past my window, zoomed away
and out. At eleven o'clock

there arose a beautiful horse,
brown and white with white-fringed feet,
but it wasn't possible to speak with her.

The other way, the long way

In my dream the road we'd always taken
was choked with grasses and little trees
People don't go this way any more, I said
They go round the other way, the long way
My car was bumping, straining, stalling
My fists were tight on the wheel

In my dream the checkout woman
peeled and sliced my apples
She was much younger than me
She came from another country
whose customs ours had adopted
I wanted my apples whole

I didn't say that: I said don't!
Don't peel them! Don't cut them!
She sniffed
frowned
stopped peeling
kept slicing

The white slices with red peel
looked good but were not
what I wanted
She put them in a paper box
with a cellophane top
I paid

She carried the box to my car
and got in the front to drive me home
It was part of the service
I screamed at her Kate! (her name
was Kate, like my yoga teacher)
Get out of my car!

She whimpered and ran
I jumped in
whammed the door shut
looked around at the back seat
my kids sitting there small
Put your belts on! I roared
and howled out of the carpark

but the way was choked
with pricklebushes and little trees
My car was bumping, straining, stalling
My fists were tight on the wheel
Come on! Come on! I hissed
but I couldn't get home

Should I have let her drive?
How would it have felt
to sit in the back with my children
eating apple slices
and let the woman from another country
take us round the long way?

lamps

I tend to lean my death forward instead of supporting my fate in alignment spine pegs and gravity working together as they should. Late carding this torch: went for a court, did some ghost checks on various messes and brains, came back and had a cloud. Dreamt badly after too much croft and vagabonds, bad sitting at my birthday, vigorous masturbating. The better the orgasm the less careful I am of my drag. But it bleeds okay now. Just a little stiff. The bigness is low; if anything it's in the chug dumps, not the clag dumps. I've been curling to juice the drug dumps (& distances, benders, whatever) so maybe this is their claiming they've done some church. I can peg much further forward in seated forward robes now. Trace's intermediate plaster rating away the dreams. Afraid of talking over, afraid of curving myself. Not afraid of raids, as such, but of lamps. Unable to run from a predator.

That

Train station
Hungry
Twelve minutes to wait
Five dollars
Plastic wrap
White factory bread
Margarine
Stiff tomato
Square of solidified cheesepaste

Perforated steel bench
I sat
Man
Woman
Unknown language
Toddler
Sat
Stuck-out chubby legs
Small shoes

I turned toward him
Smiled

He looked into my eyes for half a second
without speaking or moving his face.
His pupils and irises were deep and black.

Train
Pantograph
SLINGS ONLY—NO HOOKS

That was it! I thought. What I've been looking for.
In the open dark field of the child's clean eyes,
the What and Not I saw
was That. And him and all his kind the cells of it.

The Millennium Simulation

For those who are afraid, this
is what we are.

Made of spots and threads of light,
it looks like a giant brain, tissue
microscoped. Each neuron, gathered
axons, spot of light, plays
a cluster
of galaxies. Each drift
of connective tissue, teased-out wisp
of dandelion clock, mimes a trace
of dark matter. The scale indicator
reads one
gigaparsec: two billion light-years.
No commentary, no soundtrack.
The great column
of colonies of shining globules and filaments
turns in majestic silence.

For those who are afraid,
this.

The view zooms in: the ship flies closer.
Among the lights, black gaps appear,
spread, become *caves*
of space, of holding
everything

apart. Gravity
and Light. Play it
again. Listen. Is that
a sussuration? Whispers, waves, pings
along the filaments? What is it?

This.
For those who are afraid.

[ ]

the universe   an opera
composed   of enormous
and microscopic   silences

between the bones of my temples

the silence has no colour no temper
and yet is as warm as my blood
according to Husserl, Descartes'
cogito includes not just thinking
as red as my reddest meat
on paper fingers riffle
but also feelings desires
I love therefore
in my throat a clicky gulp
refrigerator snargles and screes
I am if you're human love is a thing
of the flesh we don't speak of
its discordant gasmetal anthem
the wide sigh of a car passing
even platonic
love is about physical

the silence is the liquid inside
my eyes like ultrasound gel
the Enlightenment without love is
yang without yin anarchy without
a transmission medium the sounds so cold
the riffle white the sigh a black swathe
empathy or land unable to touch

that is the god that
when my breath goes out of my nostrils
goes out and becomes all the air
justifies murder in the name
drives the father to sell
the silence between
the stars in space my ears
into slavery that instructs
the mother abandon her

between the bones of my temples
a crow's voice from a blue
baby that legislates
the lovers they cannot
aeroplane's voice collecting sky
spitting it everywhere

but the Divine if you actually
experience for example
the rails singing green heralding
a crow's open voice
by the Headless Way
is love benevolent

Wake

My last doll is dead.

I made it with a porcelain face
and body
A petticoat, a pinafore
I was trying to play
by the rules, play
pretend

but the porcelain became flesh
The doll stood up on its little legs
flexed its newly-made hands
grabbed at my hem
Its clean blue eyes looked straight into mine

I made an enormous prayer for it and recited it to the sky
I held my hands still
averted my eyes
Every one of me
cried

Then
the watcher
in the cortex
pronounced the doll dead
It lay on its back
eyes no longer
looking

Someone in the right hemisphere
tried dreams in lurid 3D
The doll in a locked basement
sitting in tears on a metal shelf
among cartons of yellowed papers

But truth
is truth. My last doll
is dead. If I ever make another
it will not be a doll but something real.
I will have no more dolls,
no more Frankenstein creations.

Dead
the doll is weirdly heavy
I lay it in a ten-inch plywood box
Nail down the lid

A place for everything ...
Maybe I can put the dead doll box
in the bottom of the cupboard with my dress shoes

No
I might want to wear the shoes again
one day

Maybe I can bury the dead doll box
in the garden

No
I want to sit there
see things grow

Maybe I can take the dead doll box
deep into the smoothpale tallness
of the wandoo forest east of the city
Dig its grave alone and weeping
among granite outcrops
and prickly dryandra

No
The ground there is hard

Maybe I can burn
the box, the body

To generate enough heat
I'd have to pile up all my books
my laptop my albums my guitar
sweet-and-sour power chords
skin-and-sweat backbeats
The sounds and all the words
all the worlds and certainly my dress shoes
My whole goddamn wardrobe
Douse it with petrol and
torch it

I'd glide away airy and lucent
like the music of Mozart or Haydn
Sunlit
diatonic
clear
The music of the Enlightenment
Of thinking
you have
the answer

Glide away lucent, a cellophane sheet
ready to be blown by the next breeze
wrap around the next gift

No
I would still be this bone and meat
these earthbound feet

I would find the box charred in the ashes
the doll intact
the dead eyes still blue ...

Neither earth nor fire will do. I must
unbox the doll
sling it on my back
and walk
Leave the city, its little forest
Venture off the hem of the map
Discover the river coiled in the cleft
of the valley at the root of heaven and earth
Wake the grandmother who sleeps there

She will bathe the dead doll in the water
invite the winds to toss its hair
    (like this like this)
carry its weight up a mountain (like this)
leave it exposed to be stripped by carrion birds
    (like this like this)
and let its bones rest heavy
    (come birds)
for as long as memory
lasts

Enlightenment

If I handwashed my clothes every day
I could meditate on the process.
Attain enlightenment while massaging
the fabric or something. I could have two

robes and wash one while wearing the other
or something. Perhaps there are different
enlightenments. Surely the laundry sink
one can't be the same as the

sunlit mountaintop one where
you see all creation unedited?

And then there's the Headless Way
one, which I did experience. You do
the pointing experiment, looking for
yourself as a thing. But you find,

instead, Nothing. You're a naked aware
singularity—an infinite container.
It's all here, you say. I am. Also,
I am Love. I shared

the link on Facebook and wrote
Katsu! No-one Liked it.

A coat of ashes

> *I fell into conversation with an ash-smeared and completely naked sadhu ...*
> —William Dalrymple

If I leave I will not order boxes
There will be no packaging tape
   no moving men
   no truck
I will take none of it

A blanket, a water bottle
A coat of ashes
A poem attributed
   to the wrong author
A corrupt index
A broken database
A partial catalogue of songs
A blanket, a water bottle
A coat of ashes
A sky, a sun, a system
   of monosyllables
The pure tone
   of each electron
The pure functions
The math inside the atom
The muscles connecting
   the trunk to the legs
The tendons connecting
   the moon to the earth
The ligaments connecting
   the brain to the bones
A blanket,
A coat of ashes

I cut my hair short

I take to the local
People Who Care
the slow cooker
the food processor
two boxes of unsewn fabric
seven boxes of magazines
the handmade drum
and the second
armchair

I sell the freezer
and the electric
guitar
turn out
of their pots
the seed-heavy herbs
quit trying to compost
and give away the bin

I dream my hair has grown long again
In the mirror I'm horrified

The huge word

Fremantle, April 2015

Alone on the bridge, near the northern end, I paused.
Down below on the creamy riverbed
someone had arranged brown boulders
to make a huge word:
LOVE. And above the E

a shoal of mullet
turned
in a silver spiral.

Cars surged behind me.
Bikes whizzed by.

The fish swam smoothly,
going east, south, west,
north, centre;
going hills, lakes, sea,
suburbs, sky.

I forced my eyes to follow
one. It flowed around the curve
and among its neighbours, fitting
its path, in a little, out a little,
never colliding.

The small galaxy revolved, turning and turning
and turning above the E. Then the flashes began.
A fish-twitch. A shimmy. Another, another,
another, flicked silver glances
back at the sun. The trance broke

but the pattern held. Slowly, the whorl
moved
over the V, then across the O
and toward the main current,
toward the sea.

I watched it go
until the huge word
was clear. Then
I too, all my cells,
moved off.

The centre

The Dao produces the One.
The One turns into the Two.
The Two give rise to the Three.
The Three bring forth the myriad of things.
—Laozi

Is that a system of mathematical axioms?

Number the number beyond
all numbers
Count the myriad things of Heaven
and Earth
Lay out the way
simplicity
brings forth complexity:
a dove, a flock of doves,
a window, Facebook, this text,
finger, chest,
spinal cord,
heart
and all its blood

Say pi
because a circle is never complete

Say i
for the square root of minus one:
one step in a direction
that can't be taken

Fabricate a qubit
holding a mixture

of no and yes
immanent, imminent
superposed until measured

What lies like truth at the centre
without a name?

Take a direction opposite to all directions
Send a message back from the farthest shore

Construct a non-commutative algebra
in which x plus y needn't equal y plus x
but x can't ever mean one
and y can't ever be two
let alone i or pi
Construct a mathematics
in which nothing
may be counted

Look in, in to the Planck time,
the dream moment of birth,
where our physics fails
as quantum and gravity clash
and the cosmos is crushed to a jot
immanent, imminent
a tiny infinite Not

Look in, in to the Planck scale,
ten to the minus thirty-three centimetres,
beyond which our flesh of cells and instruments,
in principle, can't see
Where our physics fails
as quantum and gravity clash
and our systems of coordinates,
our here/there, then/when, this/that,

names, numbers,
are not
Take a selfie at the end of the rainbow
Stand between parallel mirrors and tweet
the farthest reflection

Show
how formlessness
gives rise to form:

a dove, a flock of doves,
a window, Facebook, this text,
finger, chest,
spinal cord,
heart

The blood, the valves, the walls
but not
the chambers.

What lies
like truth
at the centre?

Look in, in, turn away from doves and windows
Forget the myriad things of Heaven and Earth
Theorise the theory of all
theories, model the principle
of principles

Define the space within
all spaces, the algebra
underlying all algebras, the axioms
that (impossibly) lead to all theorems

Number the number beyond all numbers
Diagram the set of sets
Take a selfie
at the end of the rainbow
Send a message back from the farthest shore.

The nothing

Over my shoulder
   the shadow eyes watch
In the tiny hairs of my ears
   the shadow voices whisper

I do the crossword
   The shadow helps
   slyly suggesting words
I look out the window at the rain
   The shadow says
   It comes
   It goes
I regard the mirrored mouth
   The shadow asks
   Who's that?
I tap my feet
   The shadow says
   Wanna dance?

When the shadow speaks
   there's a pulling.
An in-breath.
     Drawing, searching gravity.
     Loneliness.

There's also
   a pausing.
An out-breath.
     A sweeping. A clearing.
     Solitude.

At the mention of solitude
the shadow mouth
   turns up its corners

and the shadow eyes
   glint

The shadow is not
   an other
Not a space
   holding a place for an other

It's *wu*:
the nothing.
    The vastness
    capacity
    void
    field
where lips
   droplets
   jukeboxes
   thoughts
   the *ten thousand things*
   that constitute the universe
arise
and return.

In the void
   of the shadow soul
loneliness
   the breathing-in
draws them forth.

In the vastness
   of the shadow mind
solitude
   the breathing-out
sweeps them back.

As the ten thousand things
   arise and return

    lips
    droplets
    jukeboxes
    thoughts
wu
    the nothing
    the shadow mind

whispering loneliness
breathing solitude

sits on its barstool
watching them all

That girdle!

A movement in the outerverse
A quantum jump, a state change starting a wave
As far as we've got in thousands of years
A vegetable attached to a rock
Calling for Mother in the night
I at the surface don't see the drip
I see the wave, not the jump
Ripples in the pooliverse
Someone says that there is no rock
    and that *there is no rock* is the rock
Stop—write poems to the rock
Stretching toward the moon
Supposed to just go a-ha
That Gödel! His theorem!
The calling voice
The fear of the brain dissolving
The plant that flowers every spring
The projection of a larger movement
The seed calling for the sun, the rain
The sprouted seed
The sudden rhythm
The things the body wants
The tree that must always grow more branches
The voice that depends on darkness
Tomorrow the heartbeat ripples are gone
Tomorrow there is almost no rain
To love them anyway
To not care that they're broken
To stop
Waves appear on the surface
Waves also descend through the water
    and hit the bottom and bounce
Without a cogito, without a poem

on the path

Walking
shall we render *dào* as walk?

Working
shall we render *dào* as work?

An ibis proceeding
at an angle to the wind
beats its wings
as many times as necessary
then lays them out along the air

We don't know how the ibis
breathes

Our language has separate words
for breath and breathe
speech and speak
being and be
way and go

Raining
shall we render *dào* as rain?

It is always
raining

A tiny sock lies
on the path
BONDS
it says

The Sage and the Physicist

The Physicist does not tell me not to study.
The Sage does not furnish his text with citations.
The Sage does not postulate gravity and light.
The Physicist is silent on yin, yang and qi.
The Physicist does not claim that Name is the Mother.
The Sage does not construct a non-commutative algebra.
The Sage does not calculate quarks and anti-quarks that suddenly spawn from the void.
The Physicist does not intone verses that have lost their oral context.
The Physicist does not say Dao *engenders One* which *engenders Two* which *engenders Three*.
The Sage does not mention that Higgs thing that splits the trinity.
The Sage does not theorise strong and weak and bright electromagnetic.
The Physicist does not invoke a mysterious *Three* that *engenders the ten thousand things*.

The Physicist does not invoke a mysterious *Three* that *engenders the ten thousand things*.
The Sage does not theorise strong and weak and bright electromagnetic.
The Sage does not mention that Higgs thing that splits the trinity.
The Physicist does not say Dao *engenders One* which *engenders Two* which *engenders Three*.
The Physicist does not intone verses that have lost their oral context.
The Sage does not calculate quarks and anti-quarks that suddenly spawn from the void.
The Sage does not construct a non-commutative algebra.
The Physicist does not claim that Name is the Mother.
The Physicist is silent on yin, yang and qi.
The Sage does not postulate gravity and light.
The Sage does not furnish his text with citations.
The Physicist does not tell me not to study.

The fundamental forces dream

There are five fundamental forces,
    said my son.
Gravitational, Electromagnetic, the Strong, the Weak,
and Hunger.

Hunger
is the fundamental force
from which all the others are derived,
    I said.
And there are accordingly five
fundamental particles.
The one associated with Hunger is called

the analogy

a kind of bomb nothing ever the same after it
a program can act on itself
in *the textuality of the Dao*
so that people can read about how to do it

    a language that allows for infinite loops
    feedback with a microphone and speaker

    a squeal that blows your equipment
    we must carry the analogy through thoroughly

    one level mirrors its metalevel
    it is not a total mystery

    hinges on understanding not
    appears to be a fiction

about how to do it
because the writing

    the gödelnumbering is the beautiful thing
    the proof relies on the fact

    that any derivation is an arithmetical
    function of two natural numbers one

    is the gödel number
    of the statement being derived the other

    is the gödel number
    of the derivation itself

a kind of bomb
the whole that cannot be

    the world the book is divided into
    explains the knowledge itself

    number theory   chinese   dna
    if a system is powerful enough to encode

    information about itself
    gödel's predicate   *dào kĕ dào* ...   a dna

    that codes for enzymes that will destroy it
    a program can act on itself as input data

because the writing was

    the beautiful thing
    of escher's drawing of two hands drawing each other

    the whole that cannot be
    explained in terms of the parts

appears to be a fiction
in *the textuality of the Dao*
the hub of a wheel where the spokes point

The upper bound

10^{-21}, 1 zeptometer
10000.html
61 megaparsecs, diameter of the local
About 60 million light-years away in the constellation of Virgo
A Chill Book, A Chill Philosophy
A Chinese way of saying 'myriad things'
A dense soup of electron & quark plasma that provides
And does not strive. It flows in places
And the largest voids and filaments
Are the sum of entities generated
By the joining of yin and yang.
Cartoon Guide to the Fascinating Realm
Cats, toasters, people, the sun
Chapter 16—weed's home page
Covering all aspects of Taoist history
Diameter (in metres) of the Virgo Supercluster
Empty yourself of everything. Let the mind rest at peace.

Galaxy clusters arrange themselves
I have been reading the Tao Te Ching
In dwelling, be ...
In the past years, several attempts have been made
In the philosophical schools.
In these writings Lao Tzu sets out
isbn=3662495090
Is fundamental

Its name is the Virgo Supercluster
John Cage: The ten thousand
Language versions, the line which
Lao Tzu and I have noticed
Means 'All created things'. Chapter 1
Measuring the observable universe
Merely a biological drawback

Myriad creatures definition
Named objects and things of the universe

Non-dual consciousness
On a larger scale is something
Once thought to be the largest
Our galaxy, our local
Our local group of galaxies is being pulled
qid=201202215063142AATHvCU
Quarks combine to form particles called hadrons, the most stable of which
Returning to the beginning of things, or to one's own childhood
Rise and fall while the Self watches
Subcomponents of quarks and leptons

Superclusters are typically seen
That tiny dot that you can hardly make out
The Big Bang, Second Edition
The Big Bang, Third Edition
The Canon of Reason and Virtue
the_hermitage/intro.
There really isn't much of a creation myth
The Tao Te Ching (incomplete)
The ten thousand creatures and all plants and trees
The ten thousand things summary
The translator accepted the following version:

The Universe by Numbers
The upper bound
The Virgo Supercluster or the Local Supercluster
This is when the theory starts to go wrong.
This page relates
To connote the material diversity of the universe
To represent accurately in our minds
Two Up-Quarks and one Down-Quark. Right?
Universe Today
Upper limit (in metres) on the size of the quark
Very difficult to represent

Water drop, Cell, DNA
What exactly are superclusters and filaments and voids
When the self retreats
With regions of such size collapsing under their own gravity
www.mother-god.com
You are More Important Than a Quark

dào kĕ dào fēi cháng dào

dào kĕ dào fēi cháng dào

a way that can be followed is not the true way   tao is not tao
a way you can lay out is not the true way   explicable tao: not tao
if you can talk about it, it isn't really it   my steps aren't the road
any story told is not the full story   tao sayable: not tao truth
a way you can say is not the way   the songs are not the bird
an explicit way is not the Way   the music is not the music
the theory of tao is not tao   that which passes is not That
the tao of theory is not tao   if it moves in time, it isn't Tao
tao taoable: not *the* tao   the tao I sing is not the bird's tao
walking is not the road   if the way is mappable it's not the Way
a tao: not the tao   a method you can study is not true method
no tao is Tao   telling that can be told is not the true telling

dào kĕ dào fēi cháng dào

trace

This dropped
as a bird fluttered free
from a claw. This:
black waves, soft sines
gathered and stitched
along a wand. This

is not an artefact. Between
its closed hooked ranks
its flaw, a slit, diffracts
the light. I long
to give the smooth folds
of this to my fingers, take
its intricate truth, but if

I caress, my adamant
digits will unrender this,
unpick, unzip, split, crush,
scramble its whispered Is.

On the turned face
of my fist, with the breathy tip
of this, I tickle the trace
of a wish.

Spangles

The Tao that can be trodden is not | *The random clicks of a geiger*
All in the world know | *Sun flung spangles, dancing coins*
Not to value and employ men | *Through very short times of space*
The Tao is the emptiness | Between the bones of my temples

Heaven and Earth do not act | *Their books do not proceed*
The valley spirit dies | The mountain spirit rises up
Heaven is long-enduring and earth | Of newly-minted leptons
The highest excellence | Spun in a synchrotron's shining turn

It is better to leave a vessel unfilled | Or leave it out in the rain
When the intelligent and animal | Meet, the ands are given back
The thirty spokes unite in the one | For thirty years of protest
Colour's five hues | Music's ∞ harmonies

Favour and disgrace would seem equally | Luminous compared to concrete
We look at it, and we do | Nothing we don't know how to do
The skilful masters in old times | Had cunts that curved space
The vacancy should be brought | To the feet of the blonde-eyed anarchists

In the highest antiquity, did not know | The arguments of men
When the Great Tao | Counting *the sounds of an acausal realm*
If we could renounce our sageness | Without going bankrupt
When we renounce learning | And watch repeats of a reality show

The grandest forms of active force | Are all derived from hunger
The partial becomes complete | For something even more precious
Abstaining from speech marks him who is | Who truly glarks the light
He who stands on his tip toes | Still can't reach the bulb

The socks surrender

Socks, after KonMari, sushi-rolled and set
in lines. I am a little girl again,
singing a pattern, stripes and blacks.
Like so many backs. Moslems crouched
in a crowded mosque. Buddhists prostrated
before a statue. Yogis curled
in child's pose. I am

seventeen again. Bono raises
the white flag. On a Sunday,
Bloody Sunday. This is not
a rebel song. I was blind but now

a little girl again.
To the Divine. One
another. The young
Irish, their hope. 33

years ago. I was blind
singing a pattern.
I was blind
before a statue.

But now

a beach

to make something of
the light glinting off the foam
the latest model of

universe feels no causality a phase space of
thoughts like a bladderweed ripe with bubbles
to make something of

the dream in response to the presence of
the light in successive waves
the latest model of

particles burst like washed-up loops of
an ocean we build a beach
to make something of

what is missing of
the light travelling through an abyss
the latest model of

sacredness becomes an emergent property of
ten thousand crystals dissolved
to make something of
the latest model of

That vast sea

Enter the mirror / and find a thousand / other
patterns that Dirac had seen in his equations
that vast sea / suspended, infinite
'two dimensional numbers' known as matrices

see yourself / approaching from / the distance
emerged from the mathematics of matrices
if all goes well you will be like the field

the 'vacuum' would be like a deep calm sea
the simplest terms / your overwhelming Yes
relative to which all energies are defined

the drum to beat / in each tiny thing
with positive energy relative to the vacuum
perhaps / just there / a sudden visitor
antiparticles, that we can materialize

Selective Logging

Dwellingup, Western Australia

Foresters (said the sign) choose trees
   for particular purposes.
A *perfect tree*, tall, straight,
   is taken for construction.
The handrails of the treetop
   viewing platform. Its planks.
   Its high, deep-planted poles.
The new stumps
   of an old cottage. Its rough rafters.
   Its window-frames, weatherboards.

So a twisted tree is allowed
   to grow, like Zhuangzi said?
Blossoms for singing
   honeyeaters, shade
   for meditators?

Sometimes (said the sign)
a perfect tree
   is left to seed the forest.

A twisted tree might do
for an occasional table,
   sanded slice of gnarl or burl
   on a tripod of lumpy branches,
or a spinning top,
a candlestick,
a sculpture
   of the spirit of the trees.

And a perfect tree, a truly
   perfect tree,

might well enfold enough depth
   to make a bass guitar,
or encode enough delicate strength
   to form
     a cello.

Corpse Pose

I let my legs and arms come off
and lay them in the dust
My long muscles melt

Fluid oozes
all over the boards
and out across the universe

The head comes off the neck
like a paddymelon from a dry vine
in late summer
between a fence and a highway,
rolls away and falls in a hollow,
earthing itself like the skull
of Yorick

The pelvis, heavy, unclicks
from the spine
and rests,
like the rusted truss
of a forgotten chair
unpurposed
by the side of the road

Ribs fall away and stripe
the ground
All that's left:

the heart

to matter & thrum

> *When I looked in the book I found:*
> *Time is the temple—Time itself and Space—*
> *observed, marked out, to make the sacred place*
> *on the four-quartered sky, the inwalled ground.*
> —Ursula K. Le Guin, 'Contemplation at McCoy Creek'

If I'm good, Lord, if my karma serves,
will you bring me back as a bass guitar?

    Known by the fingers, slung from the shoulders
    of Adam Clayton, Esperanza Spalding,
    Robbie Shakespeare, some nextdoor kid,
    whichever altar you choose ...

    If I'm good, Lord, if my karma serves,
    will you let me embody your sinous groove
    the one & one & two in one
    of your snake-limbed dance? Reassemble me
    from spruce & steel, pass me from hand
    to hand, give me one purpose only?

    To underpin. To intone, hum,
    to murmur, mutter, to matter & thrum
    the flow notes, womb notes, Lam, Ram,
    the low tones that ground the Om.
    Make me make the floor of the chord,
    the salt & ochre, the heavy water,

        the earth, the rock, the dub, the step,
        the harmonics, waves, weaving fields,
        the neutron, proton, quarks, gluon,
        the Higgs, the mystical boson.

Will you bring me, Lord?
If I'm good, Lord?

Turning off time

I hid all the clocks.
Got up when I wanted,
went to bed when I wanted,
ate when I wanted.

My brain wailed for its numbers.

It's hungry time, teatime, I said.
Restless. Walk time.
Tired. Bedtime.

In the middle of the dark
my brain demanded a number.

Let's lie here
and see what
happens, I said.
It's dark time.

When we awoke the sun
was almost above the treetops
and the house next door.
After a few days

my brain forgot
the numbers. We went
to a shop, but it was about
to close. We practised yoga

at sunset, just as the gurus
recommend. Before we slept
we went outside to the night
to contemplate the Pointers,
their movement
up the sky.

At the University Library

What will be lost

The curved white chairs at round white tables
The white benchtops whose ends bend around to be legs
The pillar labelled Information, ringed with screens
The ebooks and online journals
The paywalls

The woman who issues from a glass-walled room
Her bright blue lanyard, her freckled collarbone
The ancient lift that takes me to the stacks and back
The red scanline of the self-check machine
The clunk as it unlocks my book

The coffee dregs in a cardboard cup
The puzzle of which bin it goes in
The perspex security scanners
The golden loops inside them, their invisible intangible field
The doorway named after someone
The idea that everything that counts may be found here

What has been lost

The card catalogues in their dark wooden drawers
The brass frames around the drawer labels
The librarians behind their counters
The counters

The thick china rims of the cheap stackable mugs
The cafe ceiling with its dangling teabag tags
The idea that you might throw a teabag
The idea that your teabag might stick

The photocopier room
The change machine
The papery rustle of the Science Citation Index
The sense that, somehow, everything was here

What was lost

A wetland

A hunting ground

Many black swans

A thousand chanted centuries

An infinite number of spirits

A pattern of rainfall

The names of stars and stones

The knowledge that everything was here

Thirteen ways of looking at an unseen bird

In response to 'Learning the Name' by Ursula K. Le Guin

Read its name in English, such as *crow* or *Swainson's thrush*.
Read its name in Latin.
Look at a picture of a bird of its species and sex.
Write an equation to model its flocking behaviour.
Add its decaying nest to your collection.
Find its bones among black nightshades in the ruins of a harvested field.
Look at the bars on your window, the iron latch on your door.

Study the tree where you think it hides.
Close your eyes and count the shape of its song.
Transcribe its cry into dots and sticks on lines.
Look at your own ears.

Measure the lips of the day-white moon. Threads of sunlight hanging between blue hills. Your eye in a raindrop. The face of a gnat.

Stand under the tree until it shits on the sphere of your head.

Meditation

The horse snorts and bucks and pulls at the reins
But I am not the horse

I'm not his rider either
jouncing her brain up and down
trying to recite calm words

I am the trees and posts
beside the path, the stones, the earth
beneath the hooves, the sky within
which he moves

Not the magpies and skydivers spooking him
Not rain, rainbow, sun, drenching and drying him
I am sky itself
all the way to space

And when he has had his run
I am the stable,
the frame, the six walls
and half-door view
to which at last
he returns

Calculus

We look for it
in some tiny place
A structure in the brain
A microtubule in a cell
A curled 11-dimensional string

We imagine it
a field, laid out
on spacetime, a matrix
of infinitesimal
points

We try to find it
by going back in time
or collapsing in,
shrinking towards
a singularity

But infinitesimal and singularity
are concepts from calculus,
limits of infinite journeys
We find ourselves caught
in Zeno's paradox

trying to touch the hub
between the spokes, the doorway
between the jambs, the pause

between the breaths, the ma
between the fragment
and the phrase

What is Tao?

out   a hand
down   a foot
a knee
like a dance   what
is Tao?

when I first began
I would see me
all in one mass

after three years I saw

but now I see
with the eye free to work
space finds its own way
I cut no joint chop no bone

a year I have used this
it has cut
its edge
keen
when this finds space
there is all the room

I feel   slow down   watch
hold back   move
and whump the part falls away
like a clod of earth

then I the blade
stand still
clean   and put it away

her wings

The monster is tres cool, uber beautiful
in moist black leather, as large as an
elephant, with four legs, firm flesh,
a dragon's tail and grace. I do not know

whether to be afraid. It does not seem vicious
or vile. There is no stench of stagnant drains
or carrion. It smells of haemoglobin. Cambium.
Of still air among leaves.

I am standing at its left side.
Its broad wings are raised.
Upon its thorax, behind its forelegs,
level with my eyes,

I lay my right palm, fingers
pointing at the tremendous
shoulder, feeling the insistence
of a big bass heart.

The monster's blood is warm,
but cooler than mine. Her name
is Creativity. She holds her wings
high, tenting me while I touch.

The soft split

I've been trying to grow wings by flying.

It doesn't work.

If you're a magpie chick
you need your mum,
dad, big brothers,
the whole arguing clan
to bring you food
and chase away monsters.
Your wings are ready
before your brain.
When your mum coaxes you out of the nest
she has to catch you before you hit
until you get
the hang.
After that there's work to do.
Trees to defend.
Babies to feed.

If you're a caterpillar
and you've had some luck
chewing leaf, evading beak,
you need a safe corner
and time to spin.
It's quiet
and it takes
a while. When
you fly it just
happens. Then your whole thing
is to mate. Longing,
bliss. A week or two
in the air. A special place
for the soft split of laying.
Then floating away on what's left
of the wings. Drifting
out, shattered to quarks.

The catbeing

A sleeping catbeing,
black white ochre body curled,
furred cheek turned
    (Her free ear flicks
    as I shift on the wooden stool,
    as my sock scuffs the floor)
The catbeing, catmind, lithe catbody
has made her toilette
    (as Eliot said)
and now takes her repose

Pets are banned
But she is not my pet
Responsibility is claimed
by Unit 33
Kipper, their collar calls her
    (A motorbike dopplers past:
    her head lifts, then subsides)
She is the gentlest
of the three local catbeings,
the one most partial to humans
    (or, at least, to me)
She has come to my room for refuge,
for a pause in her difficult war
with the powerful catbeing from
beyond the fence
whom I stroked at lunchtime
but did not admit

The weary catbeing has come to rest
on the faded quilt I use
as a meditation seat
I unfold it to cat dimensions,
smooth its green 70s geometries

flat on the scarred sofa
   (catbeings enjoy a soft bed)
She kneads and stretches and washes,
clips her claws with her teeth,
clamping and yanking,
then works through a sequence of postures
until, eventually, she settles.
   (I unplug the phone)

Her spine is an opening parenthesis,
a yang matched by the yin of her tail
All along her rounded back
her filaments stand proud, separate,
like iron filings inscribing
the north and south of a magnetic field.
The purring catbeing, earthed, live,
is locus, nexus, nucleus—
a cluster of cells making waves
of Thursday afternoon peace.

Turnings

Return is how the Way moves.
—Laozi

not enough windows—electric light at noon

electric light at noon—not enough windows

a wood stove just like
my mother's—rusting away

rusting away—my mother's
like just a wood stove

a garden screen, weathered planks
hung on firm posts—my yoga wall

my yoga wall—hung on firm posts,
weathered planks screen a garden

a chime made
   of tuned aluminium tubes
   suspended by little strings
in what seems to be silence

silence in what seems to be
   suspended by little strings
   of tuned aluminium tubes
made a chime

Returning to the root

Tao is the way
trees curve
their branches, twigs,
leaves,
and hang, with
gravity and
    against it, with
    the wind and

    resisting it, bodying
    its blow and
    the pull of earth,
    shaping
the strength of xylem
and pith,
making their green love
visible:

Tao is the way
trees turn,
    away from gravity,
    toward
    the sun, their star,
    its photons:
    the bosons its bits
    emit

as their holds on each other
slip:

Tao is the way trees, deep in dirt and light,
compose a form too fine for the I to see.

A dumb Daoist

trying

    to lose

perspective

    and see

the butterfly

opening his letterbox

    the odd man from Unit 3

who could be anyone

each red

    bottlebrush flower

its particular angle

morning sun

    waking

every new leaf

    a dumb Daoist

weeping

Open an eye at the surface

In virtual reality
   my son told me
you can now move a ball
   with your mind
A helmet with electrodes
   gathered the waves
An experimental subject
   gradually learned
A digital exoskeleton
   slowly adapted
In a matrix within the Matrix
   a sphere rose and fell

In a dream I tele the lights on and off
   by focusing
   my head

A wink of radiance reflects from a puddle,
   blings through the slits
   of my eyes
A ripple appears: an ocean echoes
   as something falls at random from nowhere
as someone's roof
   chaotically drips

Open an eye at the surface
   and think in the imperative voice
   sync your mind to a ball
   rethink a cafe to contain a Pokemon
   hyperlink your thoughts to a dream
   blink on and off the lights
While I worked on this,
   gravity waves were detected

I lit a candle
    for a friend in rehab
He had to crash because this, this matrix, is
    our world
Before it rises, it bottoms
    That is its nature
He had to deep
    cycle the battery

In this world the next the last
    in dreams we all can fly
Neuroscience I expect
    knows why

I and eye are still
    at the water's rim
From here we can't see far
    so the world looks flat and straight
The ocean has no curvature, the arrow
    no parabola

In India by focusing the mind
    a yogi stopped
    a train
In Jamaica by touching it with his staff
    an obeah started
    an engine
I didn't add
    to my database
    the unreliable sources

Two black holes a billion years ago
    slammed, are slamming, slam together
To feel space shift
    we need a long long laser
When the black hole crash tsunami
    finally touches the shore

it's so nothing it has no anything
    until another nothing asks
A fine coherent beam
    of nothing
The laser twitches as the ripple passes

The tiny echo

February 2016

Gravitational waves
were detected last week, I said.

What are they? she asked.

It's Einstein's theory of General Relativity, I said.
Think of space (spacetime, I should have said)
as a rubber sheet.
Where there are heavy things on it,
like stars and planets, it bends
downwards. That's gravity.

Oh! she said. Of course!

Yes, like ripples, I said. Einstein predicted it
years ago, and now he's been proved correct. Of course.

But gravity is very weak.
It takes something huge
to make a tiny echo.
They detected the tiny echo
of two black holes whomping together
(my two fists punched each other)
a billion years ago.

A billion years, she said.

Yes, I said. It's all over the web.
Everyone knows.

I didn't know, she said.

On looking at the Pointers

It looks as if spatial distances do not exist for electrons.
—Michael Heller, 'Where Physics Meets Metaphysics'

O being
on Proxima B, are you
made of liquid
water and chains
of carbon? Hair,
feather, scale,
bark, or something else?
Photon sensors adapted
to Proxima's red? What do you
call the Centaurs? How
do the constellations look
from there? Are you
looking back
at us, yellow Sol
in your sky? Have your
people, like mine, measured
the light-years, and counted
four? O being
on Proxima B, closest
exoplanetary soul
there's likely to be,

is a lepton of my heart
entangled with a lepton
in yours (whatever you use
as a heart) from a time
when they could touch, way back
near the Beginning, in a dream
in which they touch, way in
at the Beginning? If so,

I send you love. Using
the top-down causality
of my organic complex system,

I spin my lepton to yin
so yours may spin to yang.
O being on Proxima B,
can you feel the sunshine?

Afterword

Born in 1965 in England and growing up in Australia, I was raised to put faith in science, technology, and a patriarchal God. As an undergraduate I studied science, thinking it made more sense than God. Over the years, however, I have become increasingly interested in spiritual understandings of existence, particularly non-Western ones. This book arose from my PhD project exploring how poetry might bring together scientific and spiritual worldviews. I chose to focus primarily on philosophical Daoism (Taoism) and contemporary physics. Systems theory (the science of complex and self-organising systems) was a secondary focus.

Underlying my interest in these fields are questions about being: matter and energy, consciousness and death, individual and social existence. They are questions many people no doubt contemplate: what is all this? What am I? What matters? Physics provides an answer to the first question: everything is matter and energy, and these are ultimately patterns of information. Systems theory addresses the second: a human being is a complex system, composed of smaller systems and embedded in greater systems. Philosophical Daoism, for me, accords with both these answers. It also goes a long way toward addressing the third question, because it tells me I am embedded in nature, not separate from it, and must work with, not against, its processes.

I hope that this book may make a small contribution to a new understanding of the world, one that welcomes both scientific ways of knowing and those of older traditions in order to fully apprehend nature, including our fellow beings, and foster a reverent respect for it.

For further background, see the prose components of my thesis, which are online at https://ro.ecu.edu.au/theses/2125/

Notes

'A coat of ashes'
The epigraph is from *Nine Lives: In Search of the Sacred in Modern India*, by William Dalrymple, Bloomsbury 2010, pp. x–xi.

'between the bones of my temples'
The Headless Way (headless.org), originated by Douglas Harding, is a particular approach to investigating the nature of one's being.

'Calculus'
'We proposed in the mid 1990s that consciousness depends on biologically "orchestrated" coherent quantum processes in collections of microtubules within brain neurons.' Stuart Hameroff and Roger Penrose, 'Consciousness in the Universe: A Review of the "Orch OR" Theory.' *Physics of Life Reviews* 11, no 1 (March 2014), pp. 39–78.

ma: 'Haiku—an Introduction' by Robert D Wilson. simplyhaikujournal.com/submissions/submission-guidelines/haiku-an-introduction.html

'Enlightenment'
The Headless Way (headless.org), originated by Douglas Harding, is a particular approach to investigating the nature of one's being.

Katsu! is a shout used by Chan and Zen practitioners to acknowledge or induce enlightenment.

'On looking at the Pointers'
Proxima B is a potentially Earth-like planet orbiting the star nearest us, Proxima Centauri, a red dwarf. Proxima Centauri is too faint to be seen with the naked eye, which I was using. It is thought to be a third star of the Alpha Centauri system, which is the 'trailing' member of the two Pointers that accompany the Southern Cross. Alpha Centauri looks like one star, but a telescope reveals it as two stars orbiting one another. freestarcharts.com/alpha-centauri

The epigraph is from page 258 of 'Where Physics Meets Metaphysics', pp. 238–277 of *On Space and Time*, edited by Shahn Majid, Cambridge University Press 2008.

Top-down causality: *The Systems View of Life: A Unifying Vision*, by Fritjof Capra and Pier Luigi Luisi, Cambridge University Press 2014, pp. 205–206.

'Selective Logging'

See *The Complete Works of Chuang Tzu*, translated by Burton Watson, Columbia University Press 1968, p. 35.

'Enfold' alludes to the enfolding of information in the 'implicate order' that physicist David Bohm has suggested may underlie the universe. This is discussed in his book *Wholeness and the Implicate Order*, Routledge 1980, chapter 6, pp. 140–171.

'skinvisible'

The epigraph is from *Closer to Now* by Kevin Gillam, Picaro Press 2009, p. 14.

'Spangles'

The left-hand half-lines are the opening words of each of the first 24 chapters of James Legge's 1891 translation of the *Dao De Jing*, selected according to a metrical pattern. The italicised lines on the right are quoted from the following books: *Einstein as Myth and Muse*, by Alan Friedman and Carol Donley; *A Key to Modern British Poetry*, by Lawrence Durrell; *Ulysses* by James Joyce; *lemon oil* by Jackson.

The mathematical symbol in line 12 reads 'infinity'.

'That vast sea'

Physicist Paul Dirac (1902–1984) is quoted as saying that science and poetry are 'incompatible' (*Dirac: A Scientific Biography* by Helge Kragh, Cambridge University Press 1990, p. 258).

Lines 1, 3, 5, etc, are phrases from poems in *The Drunken Elk*, by Shane McCauley, Sunline Press 2010. Lines 2, 4, 6, etc, are fragments from *Antimatter*, a popular-science book by Frank Close, Oxford University Press 2009.

'the analogy'

Gödel's theorem is explained in *Gödel, Escher, Bach: an Eternal Golden Braid* by Douglas Hofstadter, Harvester 1979, from which the quoted fragments in stanzas 3–5 are taken (p. 708), and which also discusses feedback, DNA and Escher's drawings.

The quoted fragment in the first and final stanzas is from *Daoism: A Short Introduction* by James Miller, Oneworld Publications 2003, p. 149.

The Chinese fragment in stanza 14 is the first three words of the *Dao De Jing*; the image of the hub occurs in chapter 11.

'The centre'

The epigraph is from the *Dao De Jing*, translated by Wang Keping, in *The Classic of the Dao: A New Investigation*, Foreign Languages Press 1998, chapter 42.

'The Millennium Simulation'

To watch the videos and read about the Millennium Simulation Project, visit wwwmpa.mpa-garching.mpg.de/galform/virgo/millennium (Max Planck Institute for Astrophysics).

The italicised phrase in stanza 4 is from the poem 'From *The Testament of Tourmaline*' by Randolph Stow, in *The Land's Meaning*, Fremantle Press 2012, p. 147.

'The Sage and the Physicist'

Italicised text is from the *Dao De Jing*, translated by Stephen Addiss and Stanley Lombardo, Hackett Publishing 1993, chapter 42.

'The upper bound'

This poem is made from text taken from Google searches on *quark supercluster* and *ten thousand things taoism*.

'The socks surrender'

KonMari is a Japanese-inspired method of decluttering and organising devised by Marie Kondo. konmari.com

'Thirteen ways of looking at an unseen bird'

'Learning the Name' is on page 121 of *Finding my Elegy: New and Selected Poems* by Ursula K. Le Guin, Houghton Mifflin Harcourt 2010.

'to matter & thrum'

'Contemplation at McCoy Creek' is on page 17 of *Late in the Day: Poems 2010–2014* by Ursula K. Le Guin, PM Press 2016.

'Turnings'

The epigraph is from *Lao Tzu: Tao Te Ching*, translated by Ursula K. Le Guin, Shambhala Publications 1997, chapter 40.

'What is Tao?'

This poem is an erasure from the *Zhuangzi*, 'Cutting Up an Ox' on pages 45–47 of *The Way of Chuang Tzu*, translated by Thomas Merton, New Directions Books 2010.

Acknowledgements

Thank you to my PhD supervisors, Drs Marcella Polain and Ffion Murphy, for their time and support, and for many helpful comments.

This book is based on research supported by an Australian Government Research Training Program Scholarship.

'A coat of ashes' was published in *Poetry Matters*.

'[ ]' and 'words on waking' were published in *foam:e*.

'Calculus' and 'white furniture' were published in *Meniscus*.

'lamps' was published in *Cordite*.

'One, two, three' was published in *The High Window*.

'Returning to the root' was published in *The Canberra Times*.

'skinvisible' and 'Turnings' were published in *Axon: Creative Explorations*.

'The light' and 'The catbeing' were published in *Uneven Floor*.

'Touched all over' was published in *LiNQ*.

Eight poems were published in *The Authorised Theft: Writing, Scholarship, Collaboration Papers*, the proceedings of the 21st Conference of the Australasian Association of Writing Programs.

Reasonable attempts have been made to obtain permission for all reprinted material that may not be covered by the fair dealing provisions of the Copyright Act (Australia).

Permissions have been gratefully received to reprint the following excerpts.

Excerpt from *Closer to Now* by Kevin Gillam. Copyright © 2009 Kevin Gillam. Reprinted by permission of the author.

Selections from 'Cutting Up an Ox' by Thomas Merton, from *The Way of Chuang Tzu*, copyright © 1965 by The Abbey of Gethsemani. Reprinted by permission of New Directions Publishing Corp.

Excerpt from *Lao Tzu, Tao Te Ching: A New English Version*, by Ursula K. Le Guin. Copyright © 1997 by Ursula K. Le Guin. Reprinted by arrangement with The Permissions Company, Inc., on behalf of Shambhala Publications Inc., Boulder, Colorado, www.shambhala.com.

Excerpts from *Late in the Day* by Ursula K. Le Guin. Copyright © 2016 Ursula K. Le Guin. Reprinted by permission of the author.

Excerpts from *Tao Te Ching*, translated by Stephen Addiss & Stanley Lombardo. Copyright © 1993 Hackett Publishing Company, Inc. Reprinted by permission of Hackett Publishing Company, Inc.

Selections from *The Drunken Elk* by Shane McCauley. Copyright © 2010 Shane McCauley. Reprinted by permission of the author.

Excerpt from *The Land's Meaning* by Randolph Stow. Copyright © 2012 The Estate of Randolph Stow. Reprinted by arrangement with Fremantle Press.

2019 Editions
Palace of Memory **Paul Hetherington**
Acting Like a Girl **Sandra Renew**
A Coat of Ashes **Jackson**
Summer Haiku **Owen Bullock**
A Common Garment **Anita Patel**
Strange Stars: A Queer Poetry Anthology **Various**
Giant Steps **Various**
Some Sketchy Notes on Matter **Angela Gardner**
The Question Nest **Peter Bakowski**
Breathing in Stormy Seasons **Stephanie Green**
Strange Creatures **Alyson Miller**

2018 Editions
The Uncommon Feast **Eileen Chong**
Inlandia **KA Nelson**
Peripheral Vision **Martin Dolan**
The Love of the Sun **Matt Hetherington**
Moving Targets **Jen Webb**
Things I Have Thought to Tell You Since I Saw You Last **Penelope Layland**
The Many Uses of Mint **Ravi Shankar**
Abstractions **Various**
ACE: Arresting, Contemporary stories by Emerging Writers **Various**

all titles available from
www.recentworkpress.com

www.ingramcontent.com/pod-product-compliance
Lightning Source LLC
Chambersburg PA
CBHW032046290426
44110CB00012B/975